Adore's First Day of School

Written by Jay Lyles
Illustrated by QBN Studios

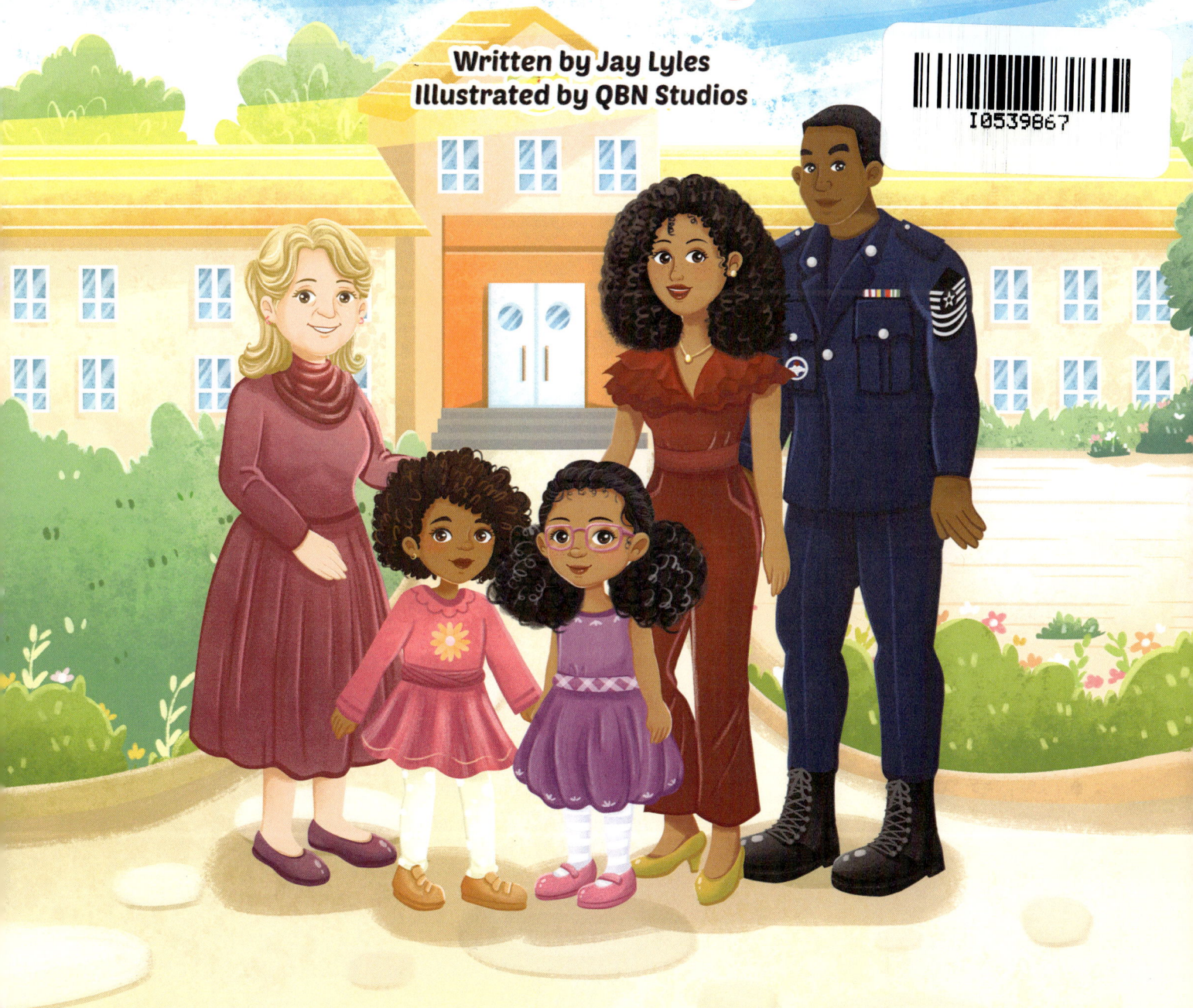

As Adore sat there on the bed
Scary thoughts filled her head

Thinking about what lies ahead
"Ah I don't want to go to school" she said.

School seems like a scary place
I don't know what to wear
I won't know anyone there
I don't know what to do with my hair

"Oh my" I need to escape
I don't want to go to school

It was then that her mother entered the room
"Rise and shine let's be on time
For you and I will be leaving soon.

"But mom", cried Adore "I don't want to go to school."

"Now Adore, we've talked about this before, school is a wonderful place to learn, grow, and so much more. Before you cry Give it a try I am sure the day will fly by."

"Mom", cried Adore I wish daddy were here for my first day,
Me too honey, but you promised to be a big girl while he was
away. The Air Force needs him now, but by tomorrow night
he'll take flight and you'll see everything will be alright.

"Off you go", says Mom
And then greeted by Mrs Tama
with a warm "Hello".

Q & A Time.

What will happen next?

Do you think Adore will have a good day at school?

Will she make any friends?

Is Ms. Tama going to teach her new things?

At the beginning of class, she met her peers. Some were friendly, some were funny,

some were shy,
some wanted to cry,
And a few were a little grumpy.

At carpet time Adore helped with the calendar and daily weather,

They sang the days of the week and ate lunch together.

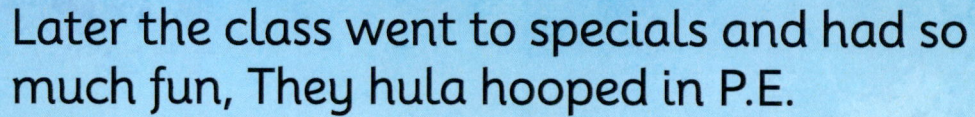

Later the class went to specials and had so much fun, They hula hooped in P.E.

For art, they drew something scary
And in music, they beat on a drum.

Adore was feeling so much better,
Making friends and learning new things,
everything was coming together.

"Once we get inside we will wash our hands for an afternoon snack," said Mrs. Tama. Then we will pull out our blankets for an afternoon nap.

As Adore began to lay down she noticed a wonderful thing. Her blanket and Vanessa's were the same.

"Go, Galaxy Go", they both shouted! And then it was lights out.

Later, from the nap they arose and the bell rang signaling for the day to close.

As Adore left the building looking for her ride, she looked across the parking lot and saw a special surprise Her father Captain Bruce Hunter stood before her eyes.

Adore ran to hug him, and he hoisted her in the air, daddy you came.

Later, Bruce came to tuck her into bed. Adore told her father all about school. At first I was scared, then it was fun, the best part was seeing you as the day was done.

Honey, I'm glad your day was sweet. School can be scary, but it can also be neat. It will open wonderful things for you to explore, but you are strong and unique and that's why you are the one that I ADORE.

Message from the Author

Hello! My name is Jay Lyles and I would like to take this time to say thanks for taking the time to read this book. Adore's First Day of School is the third book that I wrote following "Galaxy the Gigantic Gorilla" and "Jay the Jazz Playing Jaguar and His Jungle Friends". I am continuing my mission to promote that literacy can be fun for young readers.

I am especially proud of this book because it showcases my growth as a writer. This story tells a realistic tale of the fears when entering something new. I am very sure you and your little one will enjoy reading it as I have truly enjoyed writing this book. Again, I say thank you for welcoming this story to you and your family.

Other Features

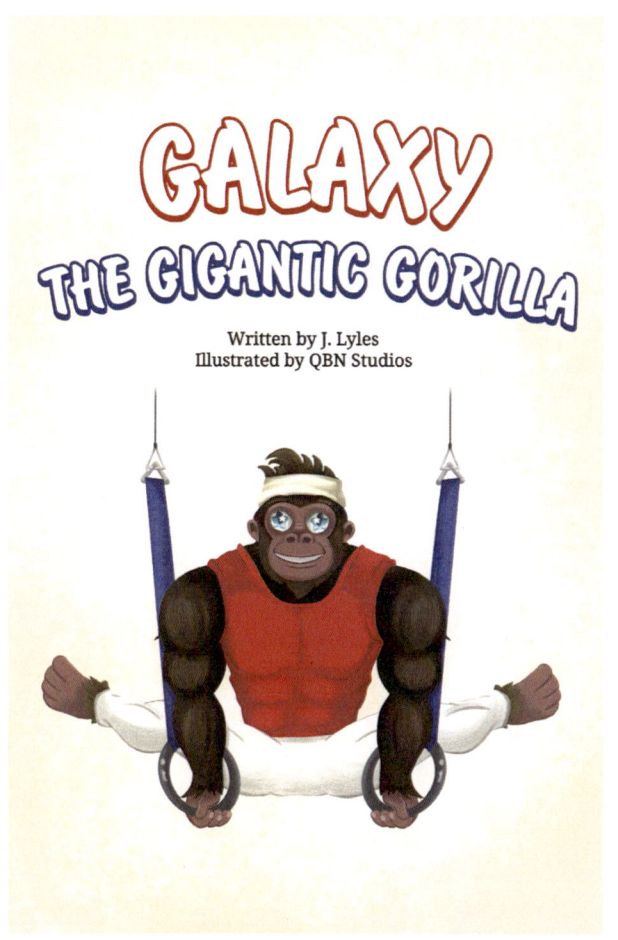

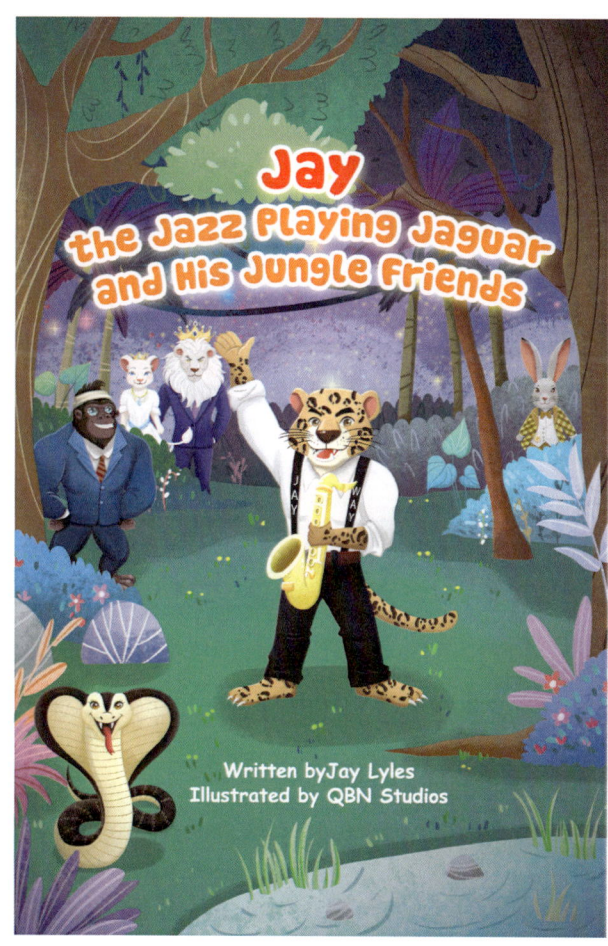

www.ingramcontent.com/pod-product-compliance
Lightning Source LLC
Chambersburg PA
CBRC090830120626
46547CB00008B/647

9 798989 185443